Self-Esteem

Cutting-Edge Approaches For Unleashing Vast Potential,
Cultivating Assuredness & Elevated Self-regard

*(Conquer Feelings Of Insecurity, Enhance Self-Assurance,
And Embrace Authenticity)*

Marcus Eastwood

TABLE OF CONTENT

Understanding Self-Esteem 1

The Prevailing Method For Cultivating Self-Assurance 7

Strategies For Enhancing Self-Esteem And Self-Confidence With A Focus On Achieving Results 22

Goal Setting Obstacles 45

Strategies Four And Five Encompass The Concept Of Cultivating Self-Acceptance And Self-Compassion 51

The Emotions Of Happiness And Introspective Recognition Are Mutually Influential. 61

Therapy And Counseling 73

Efficient Approaches To Enhancing Your Self-Assurance And Elevating Your Self-Regard 96

Understanding Self-Esteem

An enhanced comprehension of self-esteem can be attained through the examination of attributes manifested by individuals of the male gender who exhibit an inherent absence or deficiency in this regard. There exist three distinct categories that encompass men who possess a diminished self-perception:

The Withdrawn Guy

The Purist

Mister Grin

The Withdrawn Guy

This individual is widely acknowledged as a person with substantially diminished self-regard. His thoughts and actions frequently correlate with pessimism. He perceives himself as lacking capability and competence, thereby positioning himself as an underdog or someone who does not meet expected levels of achievement. His actions are frequently governed by a prevailing sense of pessimism regarding his capabilities and his character, leading him to frequently utter expressions such as "I am unable to", "I should not", "I am incapable of", and "I am left with no alternative." When faced with a challenging circumstance, his initial response is to retreat or elude. He lacks the confidence in his abilities to persevere in difficult circumstances. His thoughts are frequently inundated with a plethora of hypothetical queries, resulting in a sense of trepidation towards the uncharted territory that lies ahead.

The Purist

This category of individual frequently displays attributes indicative of a person who emanates self-assurance: exhibiting an unwavering belief in their abilities, consistently assuming responsibility, and maintaining command over the circumstances. The distinguishing factor between him and a truly confident individual lies in the other facet of his character. The purist frequently exhibits characteristics of seriousness, meticulousness, apprehension, and tenseness. He leverages his position of authority to disguise his deficiency in self-assurance. He experiences difficulty in placing trust in others, leading him to allocate tasks solely to reinforce his authority. Once the situation turns chaotic, he points at others as the cause of failure. His self-perception is characterized by such a lofty regard that he exhibits an unwillingness to entertain criticism, suggestions, or instructions. An individual who possesses this predisposition exhibits a constrained perspective of the world. He refrains from embracing novel experiences due to his apprehension of unveiling his insecurities. He adheres strictly to established procedures and views innovation with disapproval.

Mister Grin

Initially, you may perceive this individual as affable and possessing a lighthearted nature. Frequently, he portrays himself as content and takes pleasure in capturing the interest of others through his clever remarks. He thoroughly enjoys playing practical pranks and consistently exhibits enthusiasm in participating in audacious challenges. He associates his sense of value with thoughtless displays of bravery, masculinity, and manifestations of his manliness. In actuality, he maintains a facade of happiness in order to conceal his feelings of insecurity. Over time, his lighthearted demeanor begins to grate on others due to his offensive comments that teeter on the edge of racism, sexism, or any behavior that fosters feelings of superiority towards others. It is unsurprising that his foremost apprehension revolves around committing to a significant relationship, considering his inability to view himself in a serious light.

What are the factors that contribute to the emergence of such personality traits? What factors have contributed to the development of such characteristics in men?

The Prevailing Method For Cultivating Self-Assurance

Prior to proceeding wholeheartedly, allow me to clarify one aspect. The forthcoming content aims to provide you with valuable insights to construct an individual framework for enhancing your self-assurance. I cannot overstate the importance of the concept of 'personal framework.' This specific framework serves as a foundation or blueprint for your endeavors in cultivating your self-assurance. Put simply, it is necessary for you to populate this framework with pertinent details derived from your personal experiences. Only you know that.

By providing you with these overarching principles, you can subsequently tailor the specifics to align with your unique circumstances, personal experiences, and individual preferences. It is imperative that you refrain from engaging in confidence-building approaches that are generic or claim to be a quick fix. The majority of these alternatives cannot be considered as viable solutions, as what may be effective for one individual might not necessarily yield the same results for you. Consequently, it is highly advisable to operate within a structured framework. Sufficient details are discernible within the frame, evoking memories of specific occurrences in one's life. Afterwards, you may incorporate personal details and make modifications as you proceed with the implementation of the framework.

The key to effectively utilizing the framework lies in its consistent implementation. Through consistent practice, one can effectively identify the elements that are yielding positive results and subsequently make adjustments to rectify those that are not performing optimally. With sufficient execution and a generous amount of time, you would attain a framework that is meticulously tailored to suit your lifestyle. This existence belongs to you alone, neither mine nor another's. This serves as the cornerstone for achieving success.

Once more, refrain from relying on purportedly "magical" checklists as a means of developing confidence. They tend to fail on the grounds that they derive from another individual's life. Those individuals possess distinct levels of experience in comparison to yourself. These individuals might be confronted with disparate circumstances compared to yours. How can their proposed solution, when comprehensively evaluated and implemented within a commercial context, effectively meet your needs? It is highly unlikely to occur. It is attempting to force an incongruous object into an incompatible setting.

Rather, employ the structure and adapt it according to your individual circumstances. I wish to highlight this point in order to avoid the tendency to seek 'miraculous' solutions, whereby the mere adherence to certain steps or advice guarantees exceptional outcomes. They rarely do. It is imperative that you enter the setting and engage in dedicated effort. You have to customise. It is imperative to customize the solutions in order to effectively address your unique circumstances. Alternatively, if you do not choose this course of action, you would ultimately be accepting a significantly reduced amount in comparison to the full value, at most, and experiencing a complete failure at worst. With the aforementioned points stated, let us commence.

One prevalent approach to cultivating self-assurance is simply to venture forth and exhibit an air of assurance. This is the consensus among numerous other books regarding the recommended course of action. It is advisable that you promptly proceed to the desired location and exude unequivocal confidence. Simply observe individuals who exude confidence, endeavor to discern their demeanor, and subsequently emulate their nonverbal cues. What it ultimately amounts to is adopting a façade until you attain success. It is evident that you recognize the falsehood of the statement as it evokes a sensation of personal inadequacy within the recesses of your being. Internally, you experience a profound sense of inadequacy, while externally projecting a facade of unwavering confidence and superiority. You exhibit a proactive demeanor, demonstrating a strong belief in your abilities to accomplish tasks.

The benefits of employing the "fake it until you make it" strategy should be readily apparent. It is quick. The implementation process is deemed relatively straightforward. In any professional setting, it is inevitable that there exists at least one individual who possesses a considerable amount of confidence. One should simply observe that individual, analyze their behavior from a distance, and subsequently emulate certain aspects of their speech, actions, body language, and appearance. The concept of feigning competence until achieving success requires minimal premeditation. You have the ability to make spontaneous decisions. You can feel inspired by a memory of a confident person who you met in school or at a previous job. Subsequently, you direct your focus towards incorporating that individual into your present-day social interactions. It is a very free-form way of projecting confidence.

The notable drawback of adopting a "fake it till you make it" approach is its reliance on an iterative process of trial and error. As previously stated, what may be effective for an individual may not necessarily yield the same results for oneself. They might be exhibiting distinct signals and executing it with remarkable precision. They possess a profound expertise in displaying such level of confidence; nonetheless, should you attempt it, there is a possibility of facing abject failure. You may indeed subject yourself to greater ridicule.

Regrettably, the emotional wounds incurred from committing a mistake during a trial-and-error approach may require a substantial duration for recuperation. It is likely that individuals may experience emotional distress or trauma when pretending to be something they are not until they achieve their desired outcome. In the end, it is possible that you may experience a significant downfall, leading to a susceptibility to adopting detrimental coping mechanisms in order to cope with criticism. One may develop shyness or tend to exhibit pronounced judgmental tendencies. One may choose to adopt the mindset of "taking proactive measures is key to defending oneself effectively." To put it differently, your offensive or audacious demeanor appears to serve as a facade to compensate for your underlying lack of self-assurance. I am confident that you recognized the indisputable nature of these coping mechanisms, as they undoubtedly give rise to a myriad of predicaments rather than offering effective resolutions.

The significance of self-assurance and its potential influence on one's professional career.

The existence of self-assurance in an individual's character possesses the capacity to facilitate the attainment of higher levels of accomplishment. This motivation propels them towards the attainment of their goals and objectives, encompassing not only their personal life in a broader context but also their professional endeavors. Despite lacking self-confidence, individuals still have the potential to accomplish significant feats. The distinction lies in their inability to fully appreciate and derive satisfaction from their successes and achievements. They possess an insatiable drive for success, leading them to become completely consumed by work, ultimately resulting in their commitment to be workaholics. In general, it can be argued that self-esteem is the very factor that propels individuals towards success and enables them to derive satisfaction from their accomplishments.

The reality is that in order to attain success in life, it is imperative for individuals to assume necessary risks. Nevertheless, have you ever contemplated the factors that drive one individual to rise and advance, while another remains persistently restrained? Self-assurance is indeed the pivotal attribute that empowers us to transcend our limitations and embrace positions of authority, despite the possibility of encountering setbacks in the course of our endeavors. The distinction between achievers and failures lies chiefly in the degree of self-confidence we possess.

Throughout the annals of history, a multitude of individuals, both male and female, have attained success primarily due to their possession of substantial levels of self-assurance. Due to this specific factor, they assumed control over their lives and defied the constraints imposed by a stable and lucrative occupation, in order to actualize their aspirations of establishing their own business. Undoubtedly, the primary factor that enabled these seemingly average individuals to transcend their mundane nine-to-five existence and instead flourish as accomplished and prosperous entrepreneurs was exclusively the unwavering belief they placed in their aspirations and inner qualities, for the most part.

In order to garner acknowledgment, attract attention, and establish a prominent presence within your professional environment, it becomes imperative to project yourself as an individual naturally possessed of self-assurance. In order to achieve career success, individuals must possess a strong sense of confidence. There's no other alternative. Don't believe me? Please thoroughly observe your organization - what observations do you make? It is apparent that individuals who achieve success possess personalities characterized by abundant self-assurance and possess an adeptness in effectively expressing it.

It is evident that in the present times, each and every organization possesses a unique organizational culture. Due to this rationale, it is imperative that your level of confidence aligns with the manner in which your colleagues demonstrate their confidence in the workplace. Furthermore, the rapidly evolving nature of the present-day environment necessitates that you confront ever-changing circumstances and numerous conflicts. In situations such as these, your self-assurance will be especially vital and guide you through. I must inform you in advance that it will not be a simple task. Nevertheless, given your assurance, it would be feasible for you to uphold your poise and handle any arising circumstance with utmost professionalism.

An additional aspect to consider with regards to self-assurance in the professional setting is the ability it gives you to concentrate on and tackle tasks that tend to lie outside your customary sphere of comfort. It is highly effortless to acclimate oneself to a specific routine and to attain a sense of ease with particular work practices. Nevertheless, should you possess the appropriate level of self-assurance, it would be readily feasible for you to proactively advance matters and engage in tasks that lie beyond your customary sphere. An additional advantage lies in the fact that you will have the opportunity to accomplish all of these objectives while maintaining an exemplary level of grace and composure.

Individuals who possess confidence tend to achieve the highest level of success, a universally acknowledged truth that remains indisputable. Whilst in the professional setting, these individuals possess the capacity to serve as exemplary figures that are esteemed and emulated by their colleagues. Given your high level of self-assurance, you possess the potential to swiftly facilitate the adjustment of others to various changing circumstances and situations, making the process noticeably effortless. Therefore, to distinguish oneself within the professional setting, it is imperative to bring forth one's self-assurance and elevate one's performance accordingly.

In doing so, one will promptly experience the rewards of garnering recognition from employers, leading to opportunities for promotion, engaging new responsibilities, and ultimately securing a higher remuneration.

In contemporary society, competition reigns supreme. In the realm of existence, self-assurance holds profound significance and transcends being a mere advantage. It establishes the groundwork that serves as the underpinning for your ultimate sustenance. Please be aware that in the context of your professional career, obtaining a specific job opportunity is contingent upon receiving an invitation to interview. Furthermore, during the interview process, it is imperative that you effectively showcase the requisite abilities required to successfully execute the assigned responsibilities. Determining the extent of your confidence to assert yourself during the interview can be challenging, but it is imperative to project an appearance of confidence. Earning the trust will inexorably occur when you receive the telephone notification confirming that you have been chosen for the position. Subsequently, when the time comes to pursue a salary augmentation, it is imperative that you possess unwavering confidence in your professional abilities to substantiate your merit for such an increase. Regrettably, it is only those individuals who possess an optimistic disposition who receive acknowledgment in the workplace. The admiration and acceptance they receive engenders tranquility and a surplus of vigor, thereby substantially contributing to their overall efficacy. The efficacy resulting from your self-assurance contributes to your ability to succeed, ultimately leading to accomplishments that further enhance your self-assurance.

Having a sense of self-assurance is akin to upholding an enchanting vortex. How come, you ask? This phenomenon occurs as a result of developing a profound sense of self-assurance, whereby material wealth and contentment manifest themselves in close proximity. Consequently, it is imperative that you possess unwavering faith in your abilities, affirming to yourself that you possess boundless potential within you. By doing so, you will experience the splendor that life has to offer. Ultimately, individuals who possess the belief that they can emerge victorious are often the ones who achieve success.

Strategies For Enhancing Self-Esteem And Self-Confidence With A Focus On Achieving Results

Previously exemplified in the literary work, we were introduced to the significance of optimal self-esteem and self-assurance in an individual's existence. Similarly, it can be observed that the two variables hold the potential to influence the level of attainment. Hence, this section will elucidate a range of approaches that can augment both your self-esteem and self-confidence. Furthermore, given the striking resemblance between these two factors, the proposed enhancement option below will effectively elevate both factors.

Allow me to present:

Embody an Attitude of Determination: Displaying a mindset of unwavering determination is a crucial characteristic in any trailblazer. It epitomizes the notion of having self-confidence in one's ability to accomplish specific objectives. Per the adage, should you not aid your own cause, no one else shall be able to extend their assistance. This does not imply that there will be an absolute absence of individuals willing to provide assistance; there may indeed be individuals who would be inclined to do so. However, the desired change remains contingent upon the actions you will undertake individually. A substantial number of accomplished individuals have encountered diverse obstacles in order to reach their current status. And what makes them different is their capacity to infuse themselves with the 'Can do' mentality, assuring themselves that no matter what the constraints ahead of them may be, they will face it and actualize their goal.

Enhance personal competence (Self-development): Insufficient readiness has been identified as a substantial contributor to diminished self-assurance and self-assurance. Given these circumstances, it is imperative that you take measures to attend to your personal grooming in every possible manner. Will you be attending a presentation, examination, tutorial session, or a formal discussion? Prioritizing the acquisition of pertinent knowledge in advance will assuredly amplify your assurance and self-assurance to surpass your anticipations.

Gain an understanding of your strengths and weaknesses: An error that individuals may fall into is believing that every trailblazer is flawless in every aspect. Contrary to expectations, those individuals who possess great influence on a global scale also harbor concealed vulnerabilities within themselves.

However, their distinguishing factor lies in their ability to recognize and exploit their strengths in order to set themselves apart from others. Therefore, it is imperative to pause, contemplate earnestly in order to ascertain your inherent capabilities, and subsequently strategize effectively to effectuate the desired outcome. However, every weakness can be addressed. In addition to harnessing your strengths, investing effort into improving weaknesses can greatly enhance your self-esteem and confidence.

Eliminate pessimistic thoughts from your consciousness: Failure may be inevitable if one does not exercise caution, as negative thoughts possess the potential to impede success, even in situations where victory is assured with absolute certainty. Negativity is a significant factor in diminishing one's self-esteem and confidence; nevertheless, you possess the means to render its influence ineffectual in your life. The crux lies in offsetting negative thoughts through the integration of positive thoughts.

Consider your accomplishments: There are particular instances or occasions in life that often evoke a sense of unease, prompting us to ponder our deepest thoughts or question our ability to conquer obstacles. At this juncture, should one fail to exercise caution, the deluge of pessimistic thoughts surging through one's mind could potentially have a detrimental impact on both one's confidence and self-worth. However, a prompt and alternate course of action required to mitigate the negative effects is to reflect upon the accomplishments you have previously attained. The purpose of this is to instill in you the confidence that by successfully attaining a particular objective in the past, you unquestionably possess the ability to surmount the forthcoming challenge.

Exercise caution when it comes to your verbal exchanges with others: It is important to recognize that speaking at a more deliberate pace can indeed have a positive impact on one's self-esteem and confidence. The reality is that the manner in which you articulate your conversation significantly influences the level of recognition you garner from your audience. Some individuals possess extensive knowledge on a subject, however, their inclination to speak rapidly due to the hastiness of their thoughts could impede their ability to effectively articulate their point. Consequently, this may undermine their self-assurance and self-worth, potentially stemming from a perceived failure to meet the expectations imposed upon them during discussions or presentations. Do you not believe that adopting a cautious and deliberate approach in the gradual delivery of your speeches would significantly enhance your audience's inclination to attentively engage with your content?

Therefore, if you tend to encounter challenges when conveying oral information to others, it would greatly benefit you to proceed at a slower pace. This will enhance individuals' inclination to lend their ears to your discourse, consequently enhancing your morale for a more optimal experience. Therefore, you must understand that presenting your thought slowly doesn't make you less capable of having the right impact on your audience.

Confronting an obstacle is a prerequisite for individuals who aspire to achieve success.

A considerable number of individuals hold the perception that challenges should be diligently evaded under all circumstances. Do you belong to this particular group of individuals? The underlying reality is that, in the absence of life's trials and tribulations, we will remain stagnant and potentially exacerbate our circumstances. Challenge is that hurdle one must successfully scale through to experience not only the next phase of life but greater height. Consider an individual who is unwilling to participate in a promotional examination as a result of apprehension surrounding potential failure. Envision a person who harbors no inclination to engage in labor but aspires to acquire a sustainable source of income. What about an athlete who consistently fantasizes about achieving victory without demonstrating a willingness to endure the demanding trials of rigorous training? The fundamental ideology at play here is that obstacles represent opportunities for ascending to greater levels of achievement. In addition to adapting to these challenges, you are also enhancing your self-esteem and confidence, enabling you to effectively overcome future obstacles.

In addition to the aforementioned suggestions for enhancing your self-esteem and confidence, the subsequent recommendations will be beneficial and should be incorporated into your approach:

Embrace the notion that change is an immutable presence in our lives, and remain perpetually prepared for its arrival.

Make efforts to develop solutions for the needs of individuals in your vicinity.

Consistently demonstrating amicable behaviors such as engaging in smiling and reciprocating greetings, among other actions.

Express gratitude towards the individuals in your vicinity.

keep yourself physically fit.

manage your time well.

mitigate the state of being inactive

Make gradual progress towards your desired objectives; a measured and methodical approach can result in eventual victory.

don't procrastinate.

Acquiring knowledge grants individuals the ability to wield influence and authority. Given the array of resources mentioned above, it is imperative to incorporate an additional element into your repertoire - namely, discipline. This fosters a steadfast commitment to your plan, regardless of the circumstances. Finally, always remember to sustain your motivation!

4.2 Comprehending Nonverbal Communication Signals

Nonverbal communication is a primary mode of conveying information, and observing body language yields more comprehensive insights than any other communicative method. An individual's physique never deceives; when they experience disturbance, their physical manifestations will reveal it. Should they experience anger, their physiological responses will manifest. The physique will manifest the desires and aversions of an individual when they are fatigued, engaged, disinterested, etc.

Body language is part of our everyday transactions and interactions. It is highly likely that you are already engaged in the perceptive observation and analysis of a significant amount of non-verbal communication, surpassing your own awareness. Observing the rhythmic movement of the hips in another individual while walking can provide sufficient insight into their intentions and desires. A slight alteration in the direction of one's gaze can greatly signify body language. These movements, although scarcely noticeable, ultimately contribute to the conveyance of thoughts and dispositions.

If you possess any prior exposure to acting or improvisation, you would be aware that the manner in which an individual presents themselves physically can provide insights into their character. In the event that an individual "guides" with a specific body part, it becomes evident in their gait; one may observe how they walk, with one person leading with their head, which becomes the most conspicuous part of their body as they move. An alternate individual could potentially initiate movement by pivoting from the hips. Individuals often exhibit a tendency to emphasize a particular body part while engaging in locomotion, thereby providing insight into certain aspects of their character or disposition. Take the following scenario as an illustration: when an individual exhibits a forward posture with their hips, it is plausible to discern their proclivity towards sensuality and sexuality. These primal urges seem to serve as their modus operandi, governing their actions and utilization of their physical and mental faculties in their surrounding environment. Should an individual approach a situation primarily with their intellect, it is likely that they possess a preference for employing cognitive abilities to address the issue at hand. Should an individual exhibit a tendency to lead with their feet, it is indicative of a sense of caution and an inclination towards proceeding with discretion, refraining from prompt engagement until assurance of a safe and favorable outcome is established.

These instances exemplify the various methodologies by which one can analyze nonverbal cues. Please be reminded that body language is a form of artistic communication, both in its expression and interpretation. Please be mindful of employing strategic tact and judicious deliberation when approaching this situation. Formulas are nonexistent; rather, it is intuition that prevails. It is imperative that you cultivate the facet of your being which possesses the ability to instinctively discern the intentions and character of individuals, and have faith in this aspect of your cognitive functioning. There exist certain archetypes which one can identify and use as a framework when interpreting body language. These are archetypes in which individuals manifest in their personalities. Occasionally, their assertions exhibit accuracy, while on certain occasions, further details unveil a more comprehensive narrative.

Initially, there exists the epitome of a "police officer" archetype. The archetype of the "police officer" can be observed in parents, authoritative individuals, and other individuals who instill fear in us. The cop's posture is big and tall, with the chest puffed out and the head relatively straight. The core muscles of a police officer must consistently be fortified, maintaining a state of firmness, while the arms should remain prepared to swiftly reach for equipment positioned along the waist area. This specific body position exemplifies a demeanor of vigilance, assertiveness, and resilience. One could invoke this archetype to recall the nonverbal communication traits exhibited by an individual that align with these archetypal attributes. The countenance shall exhibit an air of severity and gravity. The leader may extend their involvement but remains consistently vigilant.

The subsequent archetype in body language pertains to individuals commonly referred to as "nerds." The individual commonly referred to as a "nerd" typically demonstrates submissive tendencies, particularly in unfamiliar environments, whereas they consistently make efforts to safeguard themselves. The individual displays weak shoulders that lack muscular strength, indicative of their nerdy nature. There is a dearth of eye contact exhibited by individuals of this kind. The intellectually inclined individual consistently exhibits a tendency to eschew interaction, display avoidance behaviors, avert their gaze, or physically relocate themselves in order to evade social contact with the majority of individuals in society. The individual lacks proficiency in social interaction. Nevertheless, when the individual who possesses intellectual prowess finds themselves in their preferred domain, they will exude a heightened presence and enhanced capabilities. When individuals are in the presence of someone they have confidence in or engaged in an activity that brings them satisfaction, it is possible for them to adopt an alternative personality type. This pertains to the interpretation of nonverbal cues, specifically the ability to discern whether an individual is exhibiting comfort or discomfort in a given situation.

An additional archetype that warrants consideration is the "enchantress." The enchantress assumes an attitude of possessing that which is coveted by all. They may exhibit an air of reserve in their verbal expression, yet their nonverbal cues convey a strong sense of implication. They may opt for attire that emphasizes their bodily contours and derive pleasure from teasing and engaging in physical displays, selectively revealing specific aspects to particular individuals. The individual with seductive qualities will possess the precise discernment to determine the opportune moments for unveiling their true nature to those in their vicinity, as well as when it is prudent to maintain silence. They possess adept manipulation skills and strategically exploit their alluring charm to achieve their desired outcomes. This individual's body language comprises an abundance of tactile contact and significant physical closeness. The temptress possesses the knowledge to establish an intimate physical bond with individuals whom they desire to associate with and will actively pursue connections with almost anyone they wish to engage with. They typically possess adeptness in influencing individuals, notably those who experience solitude or fear. Frequently, their movements will be initiated through the rotation of their hips or the prominence of their breasts, making them highly conspicuous within a given space. These individuals possess a proclivity for making a grand impression as they arrive. One will be made aware when they enter a room.

An additional embodiment of nonverbal communication is exemplified by the "elderly woman" archetype. This archetype captures the conventional representation of an older woman who has successfully fulfilled her life duties and takes great contentment in her achievements. This individual possesses a deep appreciation for her poise and refinement, coupled with a wealth of life experiences. Nevertheless, she does not prioritize acquiring her desires, as she has predominantly achieved her aspirations in life. The elderly woman is content and appears to be increasingly interested in social engagement. She will exhibit a heightened inclination towards maintaining strong eye contact and wearing a genuine smile, accompanied by vivid facial expressions that communicate her utmost delight in engaging with others. She will elegantly guide the movement with her hips, without applying excessive force. One aspect to take note of in the body language of this particular character is their facial expression, as individuals of a more advanced age commonly exhibit a diminishment in their emotional display.

A different exemplification of nonverbal communication is the embodiment of the "humble worker." This particular persona denotes an individual who possesses an understanding of their position within the hierarchical structure and possesses the ability to exhibit nonverbal expressions of deference towards their peers. These individuals may encompass individuals with whom they are employed or collaborating. The diligent employee seldom diverts their attention from their tasks, yet when they do, they will unveil their demeanor, which may provide insight into their inner disposition. The demeanor of a modest employee may align with their current situation, suggesting that they are the kind of worker who does not derive pleasure from interpersonal engagements. In this particular scenario, a modest employee would refrain from establishing direct visual contact and instead prioritize their attention towards carrying out their assigned tasks. Nevertheless, individuals who exhibit characteristics associated with this particular form of nonverbal communication tend to excel at maintaining eye contact, displaying a friendly countenance, and positively engaging with their social surroundings. This person's posture might exhibit a crouched position, indicative of their diligent dedication to their work. These individuals may prioritize the use of their hands, as working with manual dexterity is a prevalent fixation among this category.

Goal Setting Obstacles

Numerous individuals hold the belief that goal setting is merely illusionary and lacks efficacy. If one lacks a deep comprehension of the significance underlying effective goal setting, allocating the necessary time from one's daily routine to truly establish a goal can prove to be challenging.

To comprehend the significance of goal setting, it is advisable to peruse various literary works on achievement, wherein you will discover that the individuals who have achieved the greatest success have formulated practical objectives and diligently incorporated those objectives into their daily routines.

Even individuals who encounter apparent 'instant success' did not truly accomplish everything overnight. The successful outcome was achieved after numerous nights dedicated to diligently implementing a structured strategy.

You find yourself uncertain about the process of establishing a practical objective.

If you have previously attempted to establish a goal but were not successful in achieving desired outcomes, it is likely attributable to a lack of knowledge in the art of goal-setting. It is not as straightforward as merely transcribing a dream onto paper. Goals aren't dreams.

These are pragmatic, precise, attainable outcomes that you desire to observe. Allocate sufficient time to acquire knowledge of the most effective techniques for goal setting, in order to attain success in the process of setting and achieving goals.

You harbor apprehensions towards the prospect of failure.

Numerous individuals do not make the effort to establish objectives due to the presence of a self-limiting belief that they will inevitably experience failure. Hence, in the absence of establishing a specific objective, individuals can avoid the potentiality of experiencing failure.

However, it is important to bear in mind that the notion of focusing on planning for success rather than planning for failure is indeed pragmatic. The absence of goal setting can be viewed as a harbinger of failure, while the practice of goal setting can be seen as a catalyst for triumph. By acknowledging the fact that genuine success can solely be attained through the establishment of objectives, you shall triumph over this hindrance.

You have a fear of being evaluated negatively.
Occasionally, individuals may experience apprehension in establishing objectives for themselves due to perceiving them as excessively audacious. For example, suppose one desires to pursue a Master's degree by returning to college or wishes to embark on an entrepreneurial venture.
You have concerns that if you establish that objective and others become aware of it, they will scrutinize you severely for desiring it or for some other perceived issue.

If you are experiencing concern regarding the perceptions of others towards you, it is imperative to conduct a self-examination and overcome such anxiety. The reality is that the manner in which you perceive yourself holds greater significance than any other factor. When one ceases to criticize oneself, one will no longer be troubled by the assessment of others.

One might suggest that you have apprehensions or reservations regarding achieving success.

It may seem surprising, but there are individuals who possess a genuine fear of achieving success. They experience an excessive amount of pressure with regards to achieving success, thus hindering their ability to establish and accomplish their goals in order to attain success. They derive greater comfort in assuming the role of an individual who is not achieving success or is adhering to societal norms, rather than embodying someone who sets a goal, diligently strives to accomplish it, and is recognized as a success.

The reality is that there will perpetually exist individuals who aspire to undermine your accomplishments; however, the most disheartening aspect of existence is lamenting the missed opportunities. The majority of individuals tend to experience a greater sense of remorse for the opportunities they did not seize, as opposed to the actions they ultimately took, regardless of whether those actions were deemed as morally right or wrong.

It appears that you harbor doubts about your own self-worth in a concealed manner.

The way in which you perceive yourself is of utmost importance, as viewing oneself as lacking in commitment, success, and the ability to enact change will cause one to avoid setting goals at all costs.

You possess the exclusive capacity to exert authority over your actions, thus making you solely responsible for establishing personal objectives and cultivating a sense of self-worth.

Do you possess a genuine belief in its feasibility?

Individuals tend to refrain from setting goals due to their inability to perceive the potential outcomes. They don't believe. They fail to envision themselves completely immersed in the realm of success and fully experiencing its rewards. Due to their belief that it is highly unlikely, they refrain from making any attempts.

However, it is a fact that one cannot ascertain the certainty of anything unless they adhere to the requisite measures required to accomplish an objective. You have the ability to envision ambitious goals and strive to achieve extraordinary heights. Exerting effort holds greater significance within most social spheres than achieving the desired outcome. Moreover, it is highly likely that with sincere efforts, one will ultimately succeed.

Strategies Four And Five Encompass The Concept Of Cultivating Self-Acceptance And Self-Compassion.

Despite the admonition to individuals struggling with low self-esteem to cultivate self-love, the majority of people grappled by this condition tend to dismiss such counsel as they regard the notion as peculiar. However, it's the only love you can count on 100 percent in your life. When individuals are capable of embracing and cherishing their own self-worth, it often prompts those in their vicinity to recognize and appreciate admirable qualities within them. Please consider it from this perspective. If one does not possess self-love, how can one reasonably anticipate others to bestow their love upon them? It is impractical to anticipate individuals to harbor affection for someone whom you profoundly despise. This concept eludes individuals who possess diminished self-assurance. It is more convenient to transition from one unsatisfactory relationship to another, seeking validation from an individual who does not perceive you as a peer. It is necessary for you to elevate your standards and commence in recognizing your true value and principles in life. Cease allowing others to control the way you live your life and commence pursuing your own aspirations.

Strategy 4 - Acquisition of knowledge aligned with individual preferences and passions

Numerous individuals derive enjoyment from the act of listening to music. Additional individuals will derive pleasure from viewing an exceptional film. However, there are others who derive pleasure from indulging in a relaxing bubble bath or luxuriating with a rejuvenating facemask. It is imperative that you take a moment to reflect upon your personal preferences and commence indulging in activities or experiences that bring you joy on a daily basis. It facilitates the development of a heightened self-awareness if one possesses the fortitude to engage in such behavior and remain impervious to any external influence that may detract from the capacity to derive pleasure from one's own experiences, devoid of any accompanying sentiments of culpability. It is not necessary for it to be anything of a costly nature. Please compile a comprehensive catalog of activities that bring you genuine pleasure, ensuring that at least one of these activities is incorporated into your daily routine henceforth. You should cultivate a sense of self-acceptance and embrace your identity.

Each individual possesses an inner child, and occasionally, allowing that childlike essence to emerge proves beneficial for one's well-being. As an example, if one derives enjoyment from participating in recreational activities or seeking comfort through the companionship of a plush object, they should engage in such activities unhesitatingly. If you have a preference for engaging in enjoyable activities, feel free to pursue them. While you may not possess exemplary culinary skills, it would be quite acceptable for you to embark on the creation of a gingerbread house. Even if the outcome is less than perfect, this endeavor would provide an opportunity for your inner child to resurface intermittently. Allow him/her to do so because it enhances the quality of life and adds enjoyment.

Strategic Approach 5 – Practicing Mindfulness

Individuals who experience self-esteem challenges often engage in the act of reflecting upon past remarks made towards them, subsequently experiencing negative emotions as a result. It is inherent in their natural disposition. In this approach, one relinquishes attachment to prior events. It is imperative for you to focus and ground yourself in the current moment. This entails redirecting your train of thought to the present moment promptly whenever you notice your mind drifting into the past. Do not harbor feelings of anger towards your own self for dwelling upon past events, but rather, cease this habitual inclination promptly as it is bound to result in additional complications. Rather than that, acknowledge that you have had the thought and utilize it as a catalyst for engendering a constructive course of action. For instance, if one were to reflect upon a past romantic relationship that caused pain, it is advisable to disengage from such thoughts and instead observe one's surroundings. Please articulate the visual contents that are present within your imagination. Engaging in retrospection of positive experiences holds greater value than dwelling on negative events in one's life, and yields significant benefits compared to reflective analysis of past experiences. Cease dwelling on the past and refrain from anxiously pondering the future. It hasn't happened yet. Recenter yourself in the present moment and consistently refocus your attention whenever previous critiques emerge in your thoughts.

The concern with these matters is that by repeatedly acknowledging and allowing them to distress you, you are essentially confirming the credibility of someone's statement. Stop it. It's only a thought. Utilize it for the purpose of inducing introspective contemplation. Take a deliberate observation of your surroundings in the current present moment and notice the radiance of the sunlight. Observe the blossoms within the garden area. Observe the expressions of joy exhibited by individuals and desist from self-destructive actions that undermine the course of your life. Every time you do so, you make your self-esteem issues worse. The factor contributing to their aggravation is the overemphasis placed on the previous incident. The individual who caused you pain in the past no longer experiences distress, therefore there is no reason for you to endure it either.

If your parents displayed a propensity for criticism during your childhood, it is highly likely that they were unaware of their actions. Stop holding onto these things. Inhale through the nasal passages, and exhale while directing your attention towards what holds importance in the present moment. Substitute pessimistic thoughts with enjoyable thoughts. Observe the children frolicking in the park. Look at nature. Embark on a journey into the woodlands to witness the enchanting beauty of nature firsthand. Cease your retrospective tendencies as they are proving unproductive, promoting negativity, and fostering self-criticism.

It is essential to employ mindfulness in a highly constructive manner. My instruction focuses on aiding individuals in identifying instances in which they encounter formidable circumstances, and guiding them on navigating through such challenges. The initial step entails relinquishing the assumption that you are incapable of achieving it. The subsequent step entails soliciting guidance on the proper procedure. All individuals possess the capacity to acquire knowledge, yet there are occasions in which individuals may require further guidance. If you encounter any confusion, kindly inquire about the particular aspect that bewilders you, and refrain from assuming a position of incompetence. You have simply yet to cultivate the awareness of the company of individuals who derive pleasure from imparting new knowledge to you. They potentially derive the same level of satisfaction from offering assistance voluntarily, albeit in distinct situations, as you do from extending your own volunteer services.

In the forthcoming chapter, we shall address several imperative considerations that must be taken into account to acquire the desired level of confidence. This chapter will serve as a comprehensive review, outlining the necessary steps to achieve the desired level of confidence.

The Emotions Of Happiness And Introspective Recognition Are Mutually Influential.

Accepting Oneself

While there is a connection, it is important to recognize that self-acknowledgment and self-esteem are not synonymous. While self-esteem implies the importance or benefits we attribute to ourselves, self-acknowledgment conveys a stronger affirmation of one's own truth. When we have achieved a state of security, we become prepared to fully comprehend all facets of our being, not just limited to the positive aspects that are more easily perceived. In that role, the acknowledgement of oneself is unequivocal, along with the relinquishment of any capacity. We may recognize our limitations, constraints, and deficiencies, yet this consciousness does not in any manner impede our ability to fully accept ourselves.

In my usual discourse with therapy clients, I convey the notion that genuine improvement in self-esteem necessitates delving into aspects of oneself that one may not be presently prepared to confront. Ultimately, the act of developing a greater affinity for ourselves, or engaging in self-improvement endeavors, is largely rooted in the recognition and acceptance of our own worth. After ceasing to engage in self-criticism, we can then establish a strong sense of self-worth. What is the underlying cause for the natural increase in self-esteem when we refrain from being excessively critical of ourselves? The reason for considering self-acknowledgment as crucial to our happiness and state of well-being is precisely due to the fact that it encompasses much more than just self-esteem.

What constitutes the underlying factors contributing to our initial self-acceptance or lack thereof?

Similar to self-esteem, during childhood, we are inclined to recognize our own worth to the extent that we perceive acknowledgement from our parents. Research has provided evidence that prior to the age of eight, it is challenging to establish a clear, distinct sense of self that is independent of the influence imposed upon us by our caregivers. Hence, in the event that our acquaintances were incapable or hesitant to convey the notion that we were completely capable and sufficient on our own, regardless of our challenging and occasionally wayward behaviors, we were ready to perceive ourselves as uncertain. The genuine admiration bestowed upon us by our elders may have hinged upon our conduct, and regrettably, we have come to realize that a significant portion of our behaviors failed to meet their expectations. Hence, having an awareness of these reprehensible behaviors, we inevitably came to perceive ourselves as lacking in various aspects.

In addition, it is worth noting that critical yet compassionate evaluations have the potential to extend well beyond mere disapproval of wrongdoing. As an example, guardians may communicate to us the overarching notion that we possess tendencies towards self-centeredness - or lack a sufficient degree of beauty, intelligence, goodness, or agreeableness. . . Etc. Due to what a majority of mental health experts would agree constitutes a subtle form of psychological abuse, we tend to perceive ourselves as inherently inadequate. Consequently, we discover methods to honour various facets of ourselves in a negative manner, concealing the painful emotions of rejection induced by overly critical parents. The inclination towards self-critique lies at the heart of the underlying issues that, in our adult lives, we unintentionally create.

Given the inherent nature of the human psyche, it is exceedingly challenging to conceive of a scenario where we do not subconsciously emulate the parenting we experienced in our formative years. If our caretakers employed detrimental methods of guidance, as adults, we would invariably encounter miscellaneous means to perpetuate that indeterminate anguish upon ourselves. If we consistently experience being ignored, criticized, blamed, reprimanded, or subjected to physical retribution, we will inevitably find a means to cope with this internalized frustration. Therefore, when we metaphorically engage in self-criticism, we are often following in the footsteps of our parents. Relying heavily on their opinions, during our youth - and thus being more susceptible to their influence - we often felt compelled to regard their unfavorable judgments as significant. This statement merely alludes to the consistent attempts to belittle us. Historically, guardians have been more inclined to inform us about behaviors that inconvenience them, rather than acknowledge our commendable and refined social conduct.

In striving for a comprehensive comprehension of our current self-perceptions, it is essential to incorporate the discontentment and scrutiny that we may have received from our family members, acquaintances, educators, and particularly our peers who, grappling with their own doubts, could hardly resist mocking our vulnerabilities whenever we unwittingly revealed them. Nevertheless, it is a plausible assumption that virtually all of us embark on the path of adulthood burdened with a distinct inclination towards pessimism. We possess a prevalent tendency to attribute blame to ourselves or regard ourselves as being inherently flawed. It appears that each of us, to varying degrees, unintentionally contributes to the negative consequences of the ongoing "infection" of self-doubt.

The cultivation of genuine self-acceptance, even in the face of our shortcomings, would have been ingrained in us had our parents imparted an unequivocal message of unconditional love and support, which, incidentally, was fostered by the nurturing environment in which we were raised. That is not accurate; in reality, we must engage in the process of obtaining certification to validate our essential adequacy. Furthermore, I am merely suggesting that the act of solely seeking validation from ourselves does not necessarily relate to confronting contentment; rather, it pertains to overcoming our inclination to consistently critically judge ourselves. In order to achieve perpetual inner fulfillment and authentic tranquility as our inherent state of being, it is imperative that we first fulfill society's lofty expectations of embracing our entire selves without reservation.

Model That Confidence

I entered the room draped in my exorbitantly priced attire. All gazes were directed towards me. I garnered the attention of every onlooker. The women sought my companionship, and the men aspired to possess the qualities I possessed. This lawsuit presented considerable difficulty that I was about to engage in; however, I found great satisfaction in embracing the opportunity for growth and overcoming such challenges.

I confidently approached the judge with a distinguished smile and presented my document. I then turned to look at the man I was defending who was nervous, but I calmed him with a cheeky grin.

The opposing counsel then proceeded to assert audacious allegations against my person. The aforementioned statements bore elements of severity, yet they failed to waver my composed and collected disposition. Not one bit. I maintained visual contact with the presiding judge, followed by extending the gaze to the opposing counsel.

I subsequently proceeded to advocate for his situation. I maintained a composed and charismatic demeanor while confidently anticipating my imminent victory. I emerged victorious in the case and confidently departed the room with a satisfied expression...

I say me...

However, I am specifically referring to the character portrayed by Harvey Specter in the popular Netflix series called Suits.

It is likely that you are aware that I do not possess the qualifications of a legal professional. Why is there a discussion pertaining to Harvey Specter, however? To begin, in the event that you are unfamiliar with Harvey Specter, I would like to introduce him as a prominent legal professional featured in the television series Suits, renowned for his captivating persona.

What relevance does this have to the subject matter of this book?

Although it is crucial to prioritize being your authentic self, it is worth considering that embodying the qualities of highly charismatic individuals can be advantageous. Observing their actions, deciphering their non-verbal cues, analyzing their speech patterns, and discerning the qualities that contribute to their charisma can prove to be exceedingly advantageous as well.

In the pursuit of enhancing my confidence on a daily basis, I began observing and taking detailed observations on this particular individual. I would endeavor to outline several key factors contributing to his remarkable charisma. This encompassed his ability to maintain eye contact, his erect posture, and the unwavering conviction in his speech.

Subsequently, I commenced incorporating aspects of Harvey into my performances. As an illustration, I typically devote a minute every morning to simulate his gait and subsequently integrate this into my day-to-day routine. Now, there are certain actions that Harvey undertakes which are incongruous with my own preferences, such as the verbatim expression of indifference or disregard by saying 'I do not care'. I would not necessarily express it in that manner as my inclination leans towards empathy. However, I have acquired the ability to adopt a more assertive approach and refrain from constantly seeking approval from others.

Therapy And Counseling

Second Phase – Engaging in Therapy and Counseling

The subsequent stage in the development or restoration of one's self-esteem entails the involvement of a trained therapist. Not all individuals afflicted by low self-esteem will necessitate the services of a therapist, yet the matters deliberated upon in the first chapter can give rise to such a necessity.

The Duties of the Therapist

The therapeutic and educational functions of the therapist are essential in addressing individuals with low self-esteem. One method to enhance your self-esteem or alleviate low self-esteem, if necessary, is to acquire novel coping mechanisms. Every individual encounters various challenges throughout their life, even those who possess a considerable amount of self-assurance face their own set of issues.

Not everyone who seeks to enhance their self-esteem requires the assistance of a therapist, yet for those individuals who require additional support, the services of a therapist can prove to be immensely valuable. Their objective does not entail the client attaining elevated levels of self-esteem, as the genuine antithesis of diminished self-esteem lies in the realms of self-acceptance and self-assurance. The therapist will endeavor to assist the client in achieving a state of optimal self-acceptance.

This presents a significant obstacle for both the therapist and the client, given that the absence of self-assurance, commonly referred to as low self-esteem, typically originates and evolves throughout the course of an individual's life. It is unlikely that a resolution will be reached expeditiously.

Is it necessary for me to seek the assistance of a therapist?

What criteria should one employ to determine if undertaking this endeavor is appropriate and if professional counseling is warranted? Many psychologists view low self-esteem as a malfunction and consider it to be widespread in its occurrence. Regardless of the nature of the disorder or dysfunction presented by a client, it is typically accompanied by an underlying presence of diminished self-esteem. Numerous contemporary challenges are adequately resolved through the acquisition of self-acceptance and the eradication of low self-esteem.

It is the responsibility of each individual to determine whether their specific challenges, such as depression, interpersonal conflicts, or anxiety and panic attacks, are potentially amenable to therapeutic intervention.

We will now examine several therapeutic approaches that have demonstrated notable efficacy in addressing individuals with low self-esteem concerns.

Solution Focused Therapy

Solution-focused therapy, also known as SFBT (solution-focused brief therapy), derives its name from the fact that the therapist primarily directs attention towards the intended outcome during sessions, rather than the symptoms or manifestations associated with low self-esteem. It is a therapy approach that places a primary focus on achieving specific objectives, prioritizing the end result over the overall methodological process.

The focal point of this research revolves around the ramifications of current and prospective low self-esteem, with the aim of attaining the desired solution of self-acceptance, rather than placing emphasis on historical events and past occurrences. The therapist will collaborate with the client in envisioning a future devoid of diminished self-worth, subsequently formulating a set of objectives that will facilitate the attainment of this desired outcome.

After the client has identified the desired future they envision, the therapist will collaborate with them to acknowledge the existing resources and abilities that will facilitate their attainment of those goals.

The therapist will engage in empathetic understanding with the client and collaborate with them in order for the client to independently identify effective techniques and acknowledge their accomplishments. The therapist employs distinct questions to facilitate the client in discovering their inherent strengths. Should the therapist pose a query that illuminates to the client their effective utilization of strategies for addressing challenges they perceive as failures, it is possible that this could result in heightened levels of self-esteem.

Cognitive-Behavioral Therapy

Cognitive-behavioral therapy is an alternative method of treatment that can effectively enhance an individual's self-assurance and self-regard. This therapeutic approach is specifically tailored to assist patients in refraining from engaging in unjust self-criticism. During each session, the client is requested to discuss the most recent instance in which they engaged in self-criticism, along with the underlying reasons for doing so. The session is subsequently directed towards illustrating to the client that the criticism being expressed is unjust.

Simultaneously, this therapeutic approach will identify for the individual their explicit errors, setbacks, and vulnerabilities while guiding them towards perceiving these as commonplace occurrences. All individuals are prone to making errors, displaying weaknesses, and experiencing failures. The objective is to aid the client in perceiving these occurrences as commonplace and ceasing self-criticism. Furthermore, individuals can acquire the ability to acknowledge their positive accomplishments and gracefully receive compliments.

Subsequently, it is incumbent upon the therapist to impart to their client the necessary aptitudes essential for achievement and the acquisition of self-approval.

The Characteristics of an Individual Exhibiting Negative Disposition

The pessimistic individual often stands out through their interactions with the surrounding world and prevalent thought patterns that can readily be observed. Specifically, it is conceivable that you may discern these seven characteristics in individuals with negative tendencies who inhabit your social circle, provided that you take a moment to observe and identify them with absolute clarity. Negativity is a problem. This is a matter that requires relinquishment, and upon contemplation of these characteristics, it is likely that you will identify certain ones that align with your own behavior, at least to some extent. Please do not allow yourself to be daunted or excessively distressed by this realization. Occasionally, such occurrences take place; it is customary to experience distress, and it is customary to exhibit those pessimistic cognitive frameworks periodically. Nonetheless, it is crucial for you to possess the ability to identify them as they unfold.

Worry

Pessimistic individuals often experience a continuous state of apprehension regarding various aspects of their lives. They consistently remain mindful of the possibility of encountering unfavorable circumstances, even amidst favorable conditions that are currently being experienced. They perceive it as unfeasible to sustain and anticipate an eventual critical turning point at which everything will abruptly deteriorate. When such a situation arises, it becomes imperative to promptly identify it and undertake corrective measures. Once you reach that point, you can truly acknowledge the situation and commence the process of relinquishing your concern.

Pessimistic

Pessimism refers to the perpetual perception of one's glass as being half empty. Despite the remaining enjoyment within your glass, you already lament the departure of the beverage before its consumption is complete. In a state of pessimism, one's ability to perceive the positive aspects of situations becomes obscured. You are unable to ascertain the methods by which you may effectively direct your attention towards the positive aspects of life, nor can you tackle the approaches through which you will cultivate proper focus and collaboration with individuals in your surroundings. One will discover that no source of happiness will be found, as there consistently exists a negative aspect. Even in circumstances where you engage in activities that bring you pleasure or align with your desires, you consistently manage to transform them into challenging situations. You adeptly identify and highlight your state of distress or any unfavorable events, and promptly indulge in such pessimistic sentiments. This presents a significant issue.

Complains a Lot

Individuals who possess a pessimistic mindset or exhibit negativity often engage in regular complaints. They consistently endure concerns that trouble them incessantly, and are perpetually unable to discover genuine enjoyment in the present. Despite ultimately obtaining their desired outcome, they persist in discovering avenues to express discontent. Even if you were to present them with a cheque amounting to $1000, they would still find cause for dissatisfaction. "That does not correspond to my banking institution... Therefore, I will need to await the completion of the transaction." "Regrettably, the provided amount is insufficient to meet my monthly expenses... It barely provides any relief... Nonetheless, I appreciate the gesture." Observe the underlying grievances concealed within these statements - despite receiving an entirely unexpected and unobligated offering, the individuals managed to transform it into a subject of complaint. Such treatment is scarcely equitable and it also lacks in enjoyable company.

They exhibit a disinclination towards change or innovation.

Indeed, individuals with a negative mindset are inclined to remain firmly entrenched within their comfort zone, regardless of the circumstances. They display a reluctance or incapacity to devise strategies for exiting their comfort zone. They are likely to consistently provide justifications for remaining in their current location, displaying an unwillingness to actively seek new experiences. They will remain in their current location. Stagnant. Never growing or changing. Naturally, this is another aspect that they will express dissatisfaction about as well. They seek the opportunity to establish meaningful connections with their partners, which is hindered by their prevailing negative attitudes.

Underachieving

The individual who holds a pessimistic outlook lacks the motivation to attain greater accomplishments. They typically exhibit self-sabotaging tendencies as they consistently harbor the belief that they are incapable of achieving higher standards. They lack the requisite understanding. They lack sufficient intelligence. They hold the belief that inherent flaws within themselves will consistently hinder their chances of achieving success. In an ill-conceived endeavor to assert themselves, they merely decline to make any endeavor. They confine themselves to merely engaging in activities within their known capabilities, showing no inclination to venture beyond their comfort zone. Certainly, this poses a significant challenge to their success and overall prosperity; however, they consistently neglect to initiate any adaptation or devise effective strategies to surmount this obstacle. They would highly prefer to persist in secluding themselves within an atmosphere of negativity, allowing it to impede their progress.

They deplete the energy of all others.

In circumstances where one is surrounded by negativity, there is an inherent tendency to experience emotional exhaustion. Although negative thinkers may not have an intentional awareness of their actions, they exhibit a complete inability to generate positivity. They are incapable of generating success or happiness. Conversely, their incessant grievances, expressions of discontent, and overall pessimism leave one feeling depleted and longing for a means of retreat that may not always be readily accessible.

They Limit Themselves

Regrettably, individuals with a negative outlook are inherently confined in their perspectives. Moreover, it is indeed a grievous reality that they are more inclined to impose limitations upon themselves, rather than exploring alternative avenues through which they can attain success in their lives. Their ability to fully experience and appreciate the world is restricted. They do not experience positive emotions, and continuously maintain a pessimistic mindset.

The Impact of Emotional States on Health and Disease

Feelings play a fundamental role in the daily existence of every individual. They are essential due to their inherent ability to inspire individuals, making them an inevitable presence in our lives. Nevertheless, emotions hold significance up to a certain degree, beyond which they can be deemed detrimental as heightened feelings may disrupt an individual's regular functioning.

Continuing the duration of emotional experiences can also have an impact on the physiological functioning of bodily organs. They are hindered in their ability to fulfill their respective duties primarily as a result of the profound physiological alterations stemming from prolonged emotional states. Psychosomatic disorders arise as a consequence of severe disruptions in emotional well-being. Emotional distress can also give rise to medical conditions including peptic ulcer, migraine, headaches, hypertension, dermatological disorders, and colitis. The persistent occurrence of a specific emotion can pose difficulties in the treatment of such disorders as well.

Comprehensive Instructional Manual for Managing Emotional Responses

Experiencing emotional responses is inevitable, however, it is imperative that we exercise restraint in our reaction to significant emotions. Possessing the capacity to effectively navigate one's emotions, even in the face of commonplace experiences, is a vital aptitude due to its influence on individuals' perceptions of others and their interpersonal interactions. Consequently, individuals ought to refrain from allowing their emotions to govern their actions or attempting to repress them; instead, they should focus on developing strategies to regulate their responses. It is imperative to attend to one's emotions, as they possess the potential to intensify over time if not appropriately addressed, leading to the development of maladaptive mechanisms for dealing with them.

Listed below are a few of the measures one can take in order to effectively manage and regulate emotions.

To properly acknowledge and regulate one's emotional state, it is imperative to meticulously identify and designate the precise array of emotions being experienced in a given moment. This will facilitate comprehension of the underlying sentiment that becomes apparent whenever an individual experiences a particular state of being. It is equally essential to thoroughly observe an individual's internal state in order to comprehend their emotional state. When an emotion is designated, individuals can observe the impact of a specific sentiment on the choices they render in their daily existence.

Restructuring cognitive processes: The emotional state of an individual invariably influences their interpretation of various events. For instance, in the event that a student is experiencing anxiety, and they receive a notification indicating that the professor is attempting to contact them, they may be inclined to believe that they have performed poorly on an examination or anticipate some form of disciplinary action. Conversely, in instances of their contentment, if a comparable message is relayed, they may perceive it as a form of reinforcement for successfully completing an examination. It is necessary to employ emotional filtering in order to adopt a positive perspective towards the world. Engaging in cognitive restructuring aids in cultivating an accurate perspective, subsequently enabling effective regulation of one's emotional encounters. This can be accomplished by formulating diverse viewpoints and considering matters from multiple facets.

Participating in cognitive stimulation: On numerous occasions, individuals tend to distance themselves or frequently express grievances to others when they are feeling negative emotions. Nonetheless, allowing oneself to be consumed by such matters prolongs one's negative state, necessitating a shift towards engaging in positive endeavors as a means of dispelling the prevailing mood. Individuals should consider those things that bring them joy and strive to participate in them. For example, an individual may opt to engage in a leisurely stroll, engage in contemplation regarding positive aspects, initiate a conversation with an acquaintance to discuss pleasant experiences, or indulge in listening to melodious compositions that inspire and uplift.

Detaching emotions from behavior: Emotions possess significant influence, making their regulation a formidable endeavor. In this instance, it is imperative to grasp the indications that guide one to act in a particular manner. The ability to regulate one's emotions lies in the capacity to distinguish and manage the disparity between one's emotional state and behaviors. Engaging in any activity must be refrained from whenever an individual encounters a profound emotional state.

Engaging in regular and disciplined practice of emotional regulation skills: One of the most effective methods for exerting control over one's emotions is to consistently engage in the practice of regulating these emotions whenever they arise. Maintaining a consistent approach to managing one's emotions fosters mental resilience, thereby instilling a sense of assurance in effectively navigating a wide range of emotional experiences. By adopting this approach, individuals can ensure that their decisions and choices are made deliberately and are not influenced by emotions.

Efficient Approaches To Enhancing Your Self-Assurance And Elevating Your Self-Regard

Consider confidence to be akin to a muscular structure, analogous to any other muscular component within your physique. In order for muscles to operate optimally, they must be maintained in a healthy state. This can be achieved through the consumption of nourishing dietary choices, consumption of safe and pure water, and the consistent engagement in physical activity. This endeavor necessitates a substantial investment of both time and effort, yet attaining the utmost level of athletic capability entails significantly greater dedication.

The aforementioned statement also holds true for the development of the muscle known as confidence. It exhibits growth in direct correlation to the degree of performance demanded from it. The greater your efforts in harnessing its potential, the more it expands and enhances its utility to your advantage. The acquisition of self-confidence is hence a process that must be undertaken gradually and methodically, paying meticulous attention to each individual step and demonstrating unwavering resolve. It can be achieved by adopting the strategies elucidated within this framework.

#1 Develop Self-awareness

Know yourself. What are your areas of expertise or areas where you may have limitations? What aspects of your character or personality do you find commendable? Which facets of your personal being do you desire to alter? What factors have impeded your ability to cultivate self-assurance?

"Whilst responding to these inquiries, it is imperative to contemplate your personal sentiments or thoughts regarding your:

Physical characteristics - physical appearance, level of fitness

Emotional disposition - do you exhibit a general inclination towards happiness, affection, serenity, and personal confidence? Enumerate a comprehensive spectrum of emotions and evaluate your own emotional state.

*Intellect –skills, qualifications

Interpersonal skills – adeptness in social environments, perception of others' opinions about oneself.

*Other attributes

Please provide candid feedback to ensure the integrity of this evaluation of needs and abilities.

After discerning the deficiencies, proceed to establish the desired level of assurance at which you intend to operate henceforth. For instance, suppose you have an aversion towards conducting boardroom presentations; the desired objective is to attain a high level of self-assurance and deliver presentations effortlessly while captivating the audience.

#2 Take Responsibility

To make progress, it is essential to acknowledge and commit to taking sole responsibility for the desired improvements in your confidence, rather than passively expecting external factors to bring about the change. You alone have the capacity to foster your self-assurance. It is incumbent upon you to establish objectives, outline a strategic plan, and proceed with implementation.

Henceforth, presume that all occurrences are the result of your own actions. Henceforth, desist from holding others accountable for:

* Your deficient or inadequate self-assurance
*The manner in which individuals interact with you
Your thoughts, expressions, or behaviors
*Your failures, misfortunes, rejections

Do you have any other matters in your personal history, upcoming plans, or present circumstances?

Assuming leadership will provide you with the sense of being a unit manager, wherein you will assume the responsibility of meeting production targets, resulting in a bolstering of your self-confidence.

The third concept revolves around the principle that a person's thoughts shape their reality.

Our mental faculties shape our existence. While this statement may appear trite, it is undeniably factual. Your thoughts possess a potent capacity to mold your perception of reality. What are your thoughts regarding your own self-perception, abilities, and physical appearance? Do you tend to have a pessimistic outlook? "Are you frequently engaged in contemplation, pondering upon the following thoughts:

I regret to inform you that I am unable to undertake this project.

Pursuing that audition would be an unfruitful endeavor based on my current abilities, or I lack the necessary qualifications to succeed.

It's highly improbable that he harbors any genuine attraction towards me.

The detrimental effect of engaging in negative self-talk and thoughts is evident as it compromises one's confidence and impedes the expression of their innate abilities. However, you possess the capacity to deliberately select your thoughts and thought processes. In the present day, opt to adopt a mindset akin to that of an individual endowed with confidence, and you shall naturally experience an elevation in your own self-assurance, leading to more assured behavior. You should never entertain such thoughts or express them verbally.

*Put yourself down

*Say you can't

*Indicate that your desired outcome is unattainable.

"*Persuade oneself of one's own incapacity to acquire new knowledge

I urge you to engage in the cultivation of self-affirming thoughts and bolster your confidence through preparatory discourse. Express statements such as "I possess the capability to secure that promotion, as I meet the necessary qualifications"; "I excel at ..."; "I have a strong desire to ...".

Engage in the habit of expressing affirmation! Individuals who lack confidence often tend to respond negatively, typically saying "No" or, at most, providing an uncertain response of "maybe." Agreeing is indeed an effective means of boosting one's confidence. It provides you with the motivation to undertake actions that you might not have been previously inclined towards.

#4 Overcoming Self-Criticism

Each and every one of us possesses a pessimistic internal dialogue that undermines, evaluates, and censures our actions - frequently referred to as the pathological critic. The critic expresses dissatisfaction and censure, attributing responsibility to you in moments of failure, drawing comparisons between you and others, and identifying areas in which you fall short. It incessantly highlights your flaws, establishes unattainable ideals, and unrelentingly chastises you for even the slightest errors. If left unattended, it has the potential to erode your confidence and undermine your self-esteem. May I inquire about your occupation or profession? Engage in constructive dialogue with your critic, effectively countering their arguments. However, how can one accomplish this task?

*Disrupt the derogatory thought with a resolute refusal. Cease it! No further belittlement.

*Assess the impact of incorporating the opinions and advice of others on your professional advancement, interpersonal connections, and personal belief in oneself. Are you willing and ready to meet the required payment? This occurrence is not limited to a singular instance, but rather likely to be recurrent. Substitute the unfavorable thought with a meritorious thought regarding yourself, your accomplishments, and so forth promptly. Engage in the exercise of quelling the internal voice of self-doubt, and over a period of time, you will undoubtedly witness an expansion in the repertoire of qualities that depict you as an assured and proficient individual.

#5 Avoid Perfectionism

Allow me to share one of my preferred quotes, which epitomizes the concept that continual progress is imperative, symbolizing the greatest area of potential growth within an individual or entity. This indicates that attaining perfection is a considerably distant goal, and it is highly unlikely that one will ultimately achieve it. Hence, should one maintain an inclination towards pursuing perfection in all aspects, an authentic sense of contentment may never be attained with regards to oneself or one's circumstances.

The inclination toward perfectionism may impede one's ability to initiate action due to the apprehension of failing to meet a specific standard. Consequently, you engage in procrastination, leading to a scarcity of time, failure to attain desired outcomes, and a decline in self-confidence. What measures do you undertake in response to this situation?

Strive for an adequate outcome by dedicating the necessary diligence, time, and resources.

Take pride in a successfully completed task and refrain from dwelling on the hypothetical 'what ifs'. Strive for excellence within the limits of your available resources.

#6 Stop comparing

Firstly, it is imperative to recognize that there will perpetually exist individuals who excel in surpassing you in various aspects such as appearance, eloquence, intellect, charisma, and myriad other traits.

When engaging in comparisons, you will consistently find yourself at a disadvantage. Thus, it is advisable to endeavor to become the epitome of yourself rather than settling for being a lesser version of me. Thus, what methods can be employed to accomplish such an objective?

Merely gauge your progress by considering your own accomplishments and growth.

Take a moment to reflect upon your accomplishments and take pride in what you have thus far achieved.

Direct your attention towards self-improvement and refrain from comparing yourself to others.

#7 Request what you desire

Cease evading or accepting mediocrity. Why do you consistently display a passive attitude and remain silent in the face of adversity? Your insightful observation is indeed a reflection of your own struggles with low self-confidence.

If you experience discomfort when expressing your desires or lodging complaints regarding subpar service, it is likely indicative of your apprehension towards causing offense, appearing discourteous, or facing rejection. However, as a result, one may experience diminished self-worth or reduced perception of one's value, leading to the tendency to attribute mistreatment to others. Furthermore, it is worth noting that you have allowed the chance to rectify or enhance the situation to elude your grasp.

In contrast, individuals who possess self-assurance are inclined to assert their desires, inquire about their rightful entitlements, and avoid accepting anything less than their expectations. They are more inclined to take their chances with potential rejection rather than engage in a constant stream of contemplation that is populated with speculative thoughts such as 'perhaps I should have...' and 'what if I had...' How does one approach such a situation?

Ensure that you possess a clear understanding of your desired objectives.

Do not engage in unnecessary circumlocution. Start with 'I want..'

Refrain from issuing apologies such as 'I am afraid' or 'I am sorry but,' as they can project uncertainty and potentially result in being disregarded.

Occasionally propose a suggestion rather than issuing a forceful demand, for instance, "Would it not be more advantageous if you...?

In the event of a possible non-acceptance of your request, maintain your composure and persistently reiterate it until it is acknowledged. Do not allow yourself to be deterred by the fear of being perceived as a nuisance when you are certain of your own desires.

#8 Refuse firmly and unambiguously

It has been remarked by individuals that in order to genuinely attain confidence, one must relinquish the inclination to constantly seek approval from others. It is an insurmountable endeavor, thus why should you even contemplate undertaking it? Consenting to a request while harboring reluctance elicits heightened levels of stress, diminished self-assurance, and an amplified sense of insignificance. Individuals who possess confidence do not feel obliged to fulfill such requests. Merely because an individual solicits their input does not infer an obligation to comply if doing so causes them inconvenience. What measures can be taken to guarantee the attainment of proficiency in the skill of declining requests or offers?

Kindly decline the request in a direct and unequivocal manner.

Refrain from offering explanations, apologies, or justifications for declining.

Please provide a valid justification for your refusal of the request.

www.ingramcontent.com/pod-product-compliance
Lightning Source LLC
Chambersburg PA
CBHW050300120526
44590CB00016B/2435